W9-AND-743

MY LIFE IN TRANSITION

MY LIFE IN TRANSITION

A SUPER LATE BLOOMER COLLECTION

JULIA KAYE

Andrews McMeel
PUBLISHING®

three years in

I woke up one morning to realize my life had changed.

Somehow, after the seemingly endless turmoil of anxieties and exhaustion I had endured early on in my transition, it seemed time had kept on moving forward. Nearly three years had passed since I'd started on the path toward living a more authentic life; I'd been out and living as a queer woman in society all that time.

As I started consciously taking in what my life had become, I began to realize just how much more at ease I felt on the whole. When I looked in the mirror, I saw a drastically more feminine person looking back (and on good days I even thought she looked cute!), and when I left the house, I wasn't so stressed about the way strangers interpreted my gender expression. I had reached a point where everyone in my life only knew me as Julia and referred to me by my pronouns (she/her) without fail—heck, even strangers in public gendered me correctly more often than not. I had also found friendship within the transgender community with wonderful people who could relate about the nuances of our experiences. All of this led to my feeling a confidence about myself and what I was capable of that I hadn't previously known possible.

I had put in the time and effort necessary to grow as a person, but more than that, I actually felt like a person *worthy* of putting time and effort into. I stopped being a passive participant in my life and learned to do what was necessary to take charge. And despite a few still-lingering sources of dysphoria, I generally felt an innate sense of self-love that I never could've imagined just a few years before. Having broken down the walls I'd built up over the years, learning to better accept and embrace my identity, I'd become a version of myself once relegated to daydreams and fantasies.

Slowly but surely, the need to focus so intensely on all the life changes that had come with early transition began to recede into the background. It takes years for all of the bodily changes that come with being on hormone replacement therapy to fully take effect. As it eventually finished working its magic (with diminishing returns, anyway), I became much more comfortable in my own skin. Instead of an all-consuming force, my physical dysphoria was generally only triggered by a few specific sources that hormones alone wouldn't alter.

I can't underscore enough just *how much* being less burdened by the weight of my physical dysphoria has done for my overall well-being. As I began having more mental and physical energy to focus on my life outside of transition, I started to truly understand myself as a whole person. It's incredible that after such a tumultuous period of change life can settle back down into something resembling normalcy (whatever that is). Sure, I still had doubts, insecurities, and fears about a multitude of things, but the raging storm of my anxieties had greatly calmed.

Early on, I'd been trying my best just to hang on while doing what I could to navigate the countless stressful experiences that are all too common for people who medically transition. For that first year or so, time seemed to move at an impossibly slow pace.

Back then, each day I managed to push through felt like an achievement. I remember keeping a mental tally to track my progress as I inched my way toward a better life, all the while desperately searching in the mirror for signs of change to bolster my spirits and give myself hope. Gradually the days seemed to matter less as individual victories and I began to track my transition in weeks. As weeks gave way to months, months to half-years, I finally began to celebrate just my yearly anniversary. One single, celebratory day to acknowledge how far I had come. My life sped back up; I was released from stasis.

A big help was seeking out public figures online I felt I could look up to, people who had walked this path before me, serving as proof it could be done. I saw echoes of my experiences in theirs, and they served as beacons of hope for what was possible and normalized my feelings. After a lifetime of isolation, being able to see them had been immensely important.

I began to seek out and build community for myself, both on- and offline. Making friends who were trans who I could turn to for guidance, help, or just vent with about the minutiae of gender meant everything. I even began dating and ended up in a long-term relationship with another person who is trans. It felt so incredible to have a partner who innately understood my lived experience and could validate my feelings with a deep understanding.

And because I had opened myself up to sharing my experiences online, others who started their journeys after I did began to view me the same way I viewed those who came before me. It was surreal. I had somehow become an example of someone who did it, had been doing it, was continuing to do it. No longer was I spending my waking hours questioning every aspect of my identity, fearful and anxious about the path I had taken; I not only existed in society but was *thriving* in it.

Though I'm now past many of the early struggles that come with medically transitioning and my life is greatly improved, I'd be remiss to imply that everything is now simple or easy. I still sometimes find myself struggling with all shades of uncertainty, anxiety, dysphoria, depression, internalized transphobia, inadequacy, bodily discomfort, shame, and a very specific flavor of baggage that comes with growing up in a highly transphobic society. But we all have our inner demons to struggle with and process; I suppose that's part of the deal that comes with being human. Regardless, transition isn't about getting from point A to point B. It's an ongoing, lifelong process of embracing change.

By the end of 2018, it felt as if I had lived a thousand lifetimes since drawing the comics that went on to become *Super Late Bloomer: My Early Days in*

Transition. The way I conceived of myself and interacted with the world around me had significantly changed. I felt more like myself in ways I never had before and felt a pull to go back to making journal comics to help process this new stage in my life. I set out to make daily comics for six straight months, my only rule being total honesty about my feelings, for better or worse, no matter what.

As the project neared completion, I thought back on how much of an impact seeing people who were trans sharing the stories of their lives had on normalizing my feelings about myself. And not just stories about the turbulent early stages of transition, but the mundane experiences of day-to-day life. It had been so important to see that life really did go on; that we're just people with the same wants and needs as anyone else.

There may be more awareness of the transgender community than ever before, but sharing our stories is still very much needed. We may be a community drawn together by a shared commonality, but we all have unique experiences and journeys. The collection you're holding is a record of six months in mine.

In the pages to come I experience love, loss, grief, and more. I learn to allow myself to lean on those closest to me in times of need. I continually push my boundaries and learn more about myself every step of the way. My life becomes messy; I make mistakes and try to learn from them. Above all, I remain hopeful. I hope you get something out of it.

—Julia

DECEMBER 13, 2018

DECEMBER 14, 2018

MY LIFE IS FILLED WITH SO MANY LOVELY QUEER FOLKS THESE DAYS.

I MET UP WITH SOME NEW FRIENDS TODAY I'D ONLY KNOWN ONLINE!

FIVE HOURS HAD SOMEHOW PASSED IN THE BLINK OF AN EYE??

DECEMBER 15, 2018

EVEN THOUGH I MAY SOMETIMES HYPERFOCUS ON MY DIFFERENCES,

THE PEOPLE IN MY LIFE DON'T TREAT ME ANY DIFFERENT.

THIS... THIS IS WHAT IT'S ALL ABOUT.

DECEMBER 16, 2018

DECEMBER 17, 2018

DECEMBER 18, 2018

DECEMBER 19, 2018

DECEMBER 20, 2018

DECEMBER 21, 2018

DECEMBER 22, 2018

DECEMBER 23, 2018

DECEMBER 25, 2018

DECEMBER 27, 2018
SHE DOESN'T THINK ANYTHING OF MY RELATIONSHIP WITH LIV.
AUNT JULIA!! ♡
OR WHAT'S LEFT OF MY BEARD SHADOW.
ONLY GIRLS ALLOWED!
OR THAT MY VOICE IS A LITTLE DIFFERENT.

DECEMBER 28, 2018

DECEMBER 29, 2018
I'VE COME TO REALLY ENJOY DRESSING PRETTY DARN FEMININELY OVER TIME.
AM I COMPENSATING FOR LOST TIME? PLAYING INTO PATRIARCHAL VALIDATION?
YOU KNOW WHAT? IT'S OK TO SIMPLY LIKE WHAT I LIKE. WHO CARES??

DECEMBER 30, 2018

DECEMBER 31, 2018

JANUARY 1, 2019

JANUARY 2, 2019

JANUARY 3, 2019

JANUARY 4, 2019

JANUARY 5, 2019

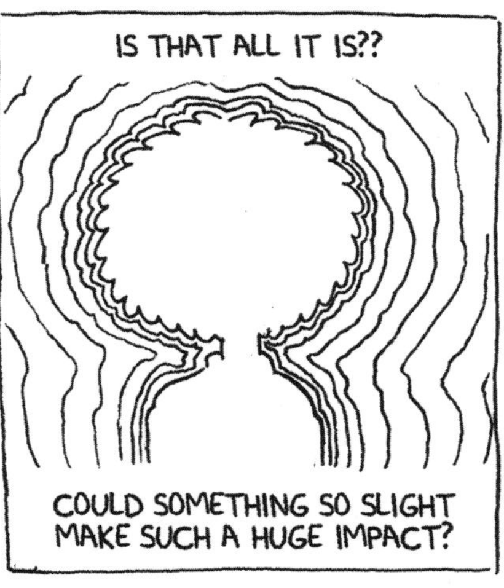

JANUARY 6, 2019

JANUARY 7, 2019

JANUARY 8, 2019

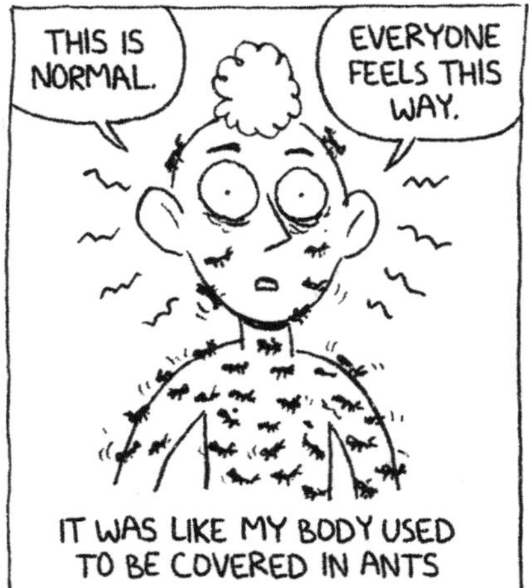

JANUARY 9, 2019

SEEING SOFT BUTCH WOMEN IN THE MEDIA AND ONLINE MAKES MY HEART SWELL.

I SEE A REFLECTION OF PART OF MYSELF IN THEM I DIDN'T REALIZE NEEDED VALIDATION.

A REMINDER THAT THERE ARE COUNTLESS WAYS TO PRESENT MYSELF AS A WOMAN.

JANUARY 10, 2019

HAPPINESS MAY BE FLEETING BUT IT'S WORTH PURSUING.

IT'S IN THE SMALL MOMENTS THAT ARE GONE IN A BLINK.

LOVING YOURSELF IS THE FIRST STEP TOWARD FINDING IT.

JANUARY 11, 2019

I FEEL TOO BIG TODAY.

AWKWARD AND CLUNKY.

I'M JUST A TINY PILOT INSIDE THIS MECHA TRYING HER BEST.

JANUARY 12, 2019

JANUARY 13, 2019

JANUARY 14, 2019

JANUARY 15, 2019

JANUARY 16, 2019

JANUARY 17, 2019

JANUARY 18, 2019

JANUARY 19, 2019

JANUARY 20, 2019

JANUARY 21, 2019

JANUARY 23, 2019

JANUARY 24, 2019
DO I WANT KIDS?
IT'S HARD TO SAY...
PRE-TRANSITION, I HATED MYSELF, SO I NEVER CARED TO THINK ABOUT MY FUTURE.
I **FINALLY** FEEL ALIVE AND WHOLE AT 30. I'M NOWHERE NEAR READY TO JUST YET...
BUT WILL I EVER BE?
I ALSO WORRY ABOUT THE ETHICS OF BRINGING A CHILD INTO THIS WORLD.
BUT AT THE SAME TIME... I THINK I'D BE A GREAT MOM.

JANUARY 25, 2019

JANUARY 26, 2019

JANUARY 27, 2019

JANUARY 28, 2019

JANUARY 29, 2019

JANUARY 30, 2019

I'VE BEEN TAKING TIME TO LOOK INWARD TO THE CORE OF MY BEING

I'M ASKING QUESTIONS AND STARTING TO BETTER UNDERSTAND MYSELF

I'M SO MUCH STRONGER THAN I GIVE MYSELF CREDIT FOR.

JANUARY 31, 2019

FEBRUARY 1, 2019

FEBRUARY 2, 2019

FEBRUARY 3, 2019

FEBRUARY 4, 2019

FEBRUARY 5, 2019

FEBRUARY 6, 2019

FEBRUARY 7, 2019

FEBRUARY 8, 2019

FEBRUARY 9, 2019

FEBRUARY 10, 2019

FEBRUARY 11, 2019

FEBRUARY 12, 2019

FEBRUARY 13, 2019

FEBRUARY 14, 2019

FEBRUARY 15, 2019

FEBRUARY 16, 2019

FEBRUARY 17, 2019

FEBRUARY 18, 2019

FEBRUARY 19, 2019

FEBRUARY 20, 2019

FEBRUARY 21, 2019

FEBRUARY 22, 2019

FEBRUARY 25, 2019

FEBRUARY 26, 2019

FEBRUARY 27, 2019

FEBRUARY 28, 2019

MARCH 1, 2019

HEY, SARA? KINDA RANDOM, BUT UH, IF I DIE BEFORE YOU, COULD YOU ENSURE I'M NOT MISGENDERED OR DEADNAMED AT MY FUNERAL?
IT'S KIND OF A FEAR OF MINE.

I MEAN, I'M **SURE** IT'LL BE FINE, BUT... I'M NOT AS CLOSE WITH OUR FAMILY AS I USED TO BE AND THEY MOSTLY KNEW ME **BEFORE**...

Y'KNOW, LIKE, PRETRANSITION.

IT'S JUST, THAT'S **NOT** WHO I AM. I'VE WORKED SO HARD TO ACCEPT AND GROW INTO MYSELF AND I DON'T WANT THAT ERASED.
THANKS. I LOVE YOU.

MARCH 2, 2019

I SPENT THE AFTERNOON DOING TAX-FILING PREPARATION
BLEHHH
I LOOKED THROUGH ALL OF LAST YEAR'S BANK STATEMENTS.

...THIS READS AS A TIMELINE OF ALL THE DATES AND OUTINGS LIV AND I WENT ON LAST YEAR.
CLICK
CLICK
CLICK

DOING TAXES IS BAD ENOUGH... I CAN'T SEEM TO ESCAPE HER.
SIGHHH...
CLICK
CLICK
CLICK

MARCH 3, 2019

MARCH 4, 2019

TH-THAT CAN'T BE RIGHT...
I CAN'T BELIEVE IT'S ALREADY MARCH.

THE PAST TWO MONTHS WERE A TOTAL BLUR...

TIME SURE FLIES WHEN YOU'RE HAVING [A TOUGH TIME COPING POST-BREAKUP SO YOU RELENTLESSLY KEEP AS BUSY AS POSSIBLE]!!

MARCH 5, 2019

HI THERE!
YOU HAVE CURLS LIKE ME! ARE YOU A PRINCESS TOO??
SNOW WHITE VISITED WORK!
YES! I AM!!

MARCH 6, 2019

I'D NEVER USE A STAR TREK TELEPORTER. YOU DIE AND A COPY OF YOURSELF IS REASSEMBLED?? NO THANKS!

PSH. SEE THAT STORE OVER THERE? I'D TELEPORT INSIDE, WAVE TO YOU, AND TELEPORT BACK JUST BECAUSE I COULD.
WHAT?!
HA
HA
HA
HA

MARCH 7, 2019

THE ONLY TIME MY DIPLOMA WAS EVER USED WAS WHEN I GOT A JOB ON WALL STREET!
HAHA THAT WAS WEIRD.
IT'S SURREAL TO TALK TO COLLEGE STUDENTS ABOUT MY CAREER. I HAVE A CAREER NOW?

LET'S TALK ABOUT SOCIAL MEDIA AND LATE-STAGE CAPITALISM!!
HOP!
BUT... I GUESS I'VE BEEN WORKING MY WAY TOWARD ONE BIT BY BIT FOR YEARS NOW.

TIME MANAGEMENT!! BURNOUT!! STRETCH!! SELF-CARE!!!
I DUNNO HOW MUCH OF WHAT I HAVE TO SAY IS USEFUL, BUT I TRIED TO RELAY WHAT I'VE LEARNED.

MARCH 8, 2019

DOCTOR'S OFFICE WAITING ROOM
IS... IS THAT LIV?? OH GOD. IT IS.
I SHOULD GO OVER TO SAY HI. IT'D BE WEIRD TO PRETEND LIKE I DIDN'T SEE HER. SHE'S RIGHT THERE.
RIGHT? ALSO, MAYBE IT COULD BE NICE...?
BLAH
BLAH
BLAH
BLAH
BLAH
BLAH
...CRAP. THIS FEELS BAD.

MARCH 9, 2019

LIV
IDK, I NEED SPACE I GUESS... THAT TIME I WENT OVER TO YOUR PLACE REALLY MESSED ME UP...
I SHOULDN'T HAVE MET UP WITH LIV A COUPLE WEEKS BACK. IT WAS WAY TOO SOON.

FRICK FRICK FRICK FRICK FRICK FRICK FRICK FRICK FRICK
MY EMOTIONS WERE TOO RAW. SHE DIDN'T DESERVE TO ENDURE MY VENTING AT HER.

I KNOW AN APOLOGY ISN'T MUCH, BUT I HOPE IT HELPS EVEN A LITTLE BIT...
TAP TAPPA TAP
IN SEEKING CATHARSIS, I HURT SOMEONE I CARE ABOUT AND IT'S EATING ME UP INSIDE.

MARCH 10, 2019

MARCH 11, 2019

MARCH 12, 2019

MARCH 13, 2019

MARCH 14, 2019

MARCH 15, 2019

MARCH 16, 2019

MARCH 17, 2019

MARCH 18, 2019

MARCH 19, 2019

COME ON, JULIA. YOU DO WANNA GO HOME... RIGHT??

MY ANXIETIES RUN AMOK AS I TRY TO CONVINCE MYSELF TO BOOK A FLIGHT HOME FOR PASSOVER.

...REMEMBER WHEN YOU CAME OUT AND SAID HE WAS SUPPORTIVE? JUST BEFORE CUTTING OFF CONTACT??

MY ANGER WELLS UP AS I PICTURE HIM PRETENDING I DON'T EVEN EXIST WHILE IN THE SAME ROOM AS HIM...

...MAYBE I'LL... THINK ABOUT IT A BIT FIRST.

AND DREAD AS I PICTURE THE REST OF MY FAMILY TURNING A BLIND EYE TO IT ALL.

MARCH 20, 2019

MARCH 22, 2019

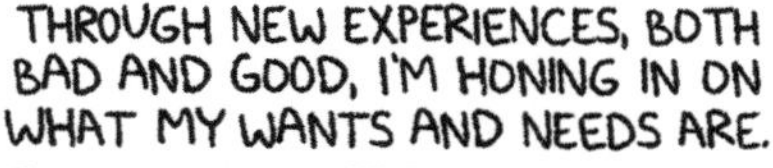

MARCH 23, 2019

MARCH 24, 2019

MARCH 25, 2019

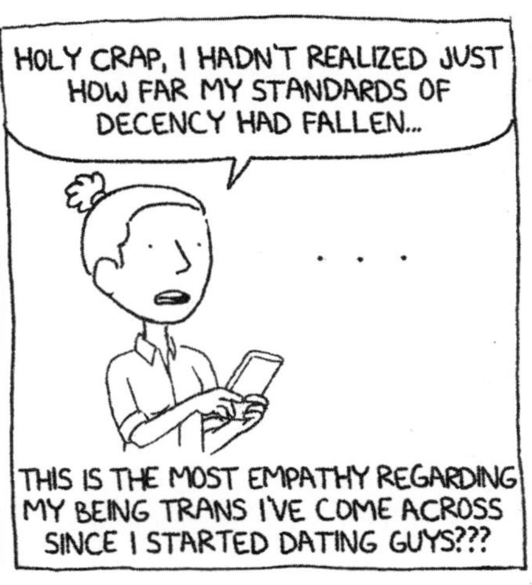

MARCH 26, 2019

MARCH 27, 2019

MARCH 28, 2019

MARCH 29, 2019

MARCH 30, 2019

MARCH 31, 2019

APRIL 1, 2019

CASUAL DATING IS EXHAUSTING... I DON'T THINK I'M BUILT FOR IT.
I JUST... WANT SOMETHING STABLE AND LONG TERM.
OH MY GOD I JUST INVENTED A COMMITTED RELATIONSHIP.

APRIL 2, 2019

HEY JULIA, I WAS JUST THINKIN' ABOUT HOW I NEVER GOT BACK TO YOU... :/
HUH. A LIST OF REASONS HE GHOSTED ME A MONTH BACK.

I... DESERVE TO BE TREATED BETTER THAN THIS.
...HUH. GROWTH.
SO I SHUT HIM DOWN DESPITE HOW FLIPPIN' HOT HE WAS.

OK, **UNIVERSE!** NOW IT'S **YOUR** TURN TO DO **ME** A SOLID!!!
TAP TAPPA TAP

APRIL 3, 2019

I'M A FEW MONTHS OUT OF A RELATIONSHIP RIGHT NOW...
OOF, THAT'S ROUGH. I START MAKING **BAD** DECISIONS TOO LONG OUT OF A RELATIONSHIP.
MONICA! THAT'S **EXACTLY** WHERE I'M AT RIGHT NOW!!
I'M LIKE THE **MAYOR** OF BAD DECISIONS TOWN!!
IT'S OKAY. WE ALL END UP THERE.
...REALLY?
THANKS, MONICA.
LISTEN, DATING IS **ROUGH.**

APRIL 4, 2019

AT A TRENDY COFFEE SHOP SURROUNDED BY BEAUTIFUL MEN
I CONSIDER MYSELF PAN, BUT MY ATTRACTION SEEMS TO BE FOCUSED ON MEN RIGHT NOW. DUNNO WHY.

BLAH BLAH BLAH
SNEAKY GLANCE
MAYBE IT HAS TO DO WITH HOW MUCH SHAME I USED TO FEEL FOR MY ATTRACTION.

SIGHHHHH~ GOD I WANT A BOYFRIEND...
IT'S INTOXICATING TO HAVE RID MYSELF OF SUCH AWFUL SOCIAL PROGRAMMING.

APRIL 5, 2019

DEEP BREATHS, JULIA. YOU GOT THIS.
I TOOK THE MORNING TO GO TO AN LGBTQ COMMUNITY SPACE DESPITE LIV POTENTIALLY BEING THERE.

HEY THERE! ARE YOU A CARTOONIST TOO? WHAT'S YOUR NAME?
YEAH! I'M LEX.
WANNA SIT?
I CAN'T LET THE ANXIETY OF RUNNING INTO HER DICTATE MY LIFE.

...AND IT TURNS OUT A SPIDER WAS CRAWLING ON MY FACE!!
AW WHAT!! GROSSSSS.
AN UNEXPECTED AWKWARD MOMENT WOULDN'T BE THE END OF THE WORLD.

APRIL 6, 2019

I CAN'T WAIT TO SHOW YOU THIS VIEW, JULIE! IT'S SO BEAUTIFUL!!
WAIT... THIS IS THE ROAD TO LIV'S PLACE?? OH GOD OH GOD OH
I WAS INSTANTLY ON THE VERGE OF TEARS.

OH SHOOT! WE CAN GO ELSEWHERE!!
NO! IT'S JUST... UNEXPECTED... LET'S, KEEP GOING.
I HADN'T REALIZED HOW MUCH IT WOULD AFFECT ME.

THIS... IS INCREDIBLE.
THANK YOU FOR SHARING IT WITH ME, NAT.
BUT... IT'S OK. I'M GONNA BE JUST FINE.

APRIL 7, 2019

IS ASKING MY FAMILY TO STAND BY ME ABOUT ████ TOO MUCH?? IT FEELS LIKE AN ULTIMATUM.

IT'S NOT AN ULTIMATUM, YOU'RE JUST SETTING BOUNDARIES.
THERE'S A DIFFERENCE.

HM... I GUESS... I JUST WONDER IF THIS WILL CHANGE ANYTHING.
I HOPE IT DOES.

APRIL 8, 2019

SO I'VE GOT SOMETHING... UNPLEASANT TO DISCUSS.
IT'S BEEN 3 YEARS SINCE I CAME OUT TO ■■■■. 3 YEARS SINCE HE LAST SPOKE TO ME.
I... YEAH... YOU KNOW WHERE THIS IS HEADING...
WE HAD ALL HOPED HE JUST NEEDED TIME TO PROCESS, THAT HE WOULD COME AROUND IN TIME.
THE ELEPHANT IN THE ROOM...
I DON'T BLAME ANYONE FOR IGNORING THE SITUATION, BUT ACKNOWLEDGING IT IS OVERDUE.

APRIL 9, 2019

IT TAKES TWO TO TANGO.
SO ON ONE HAND, THERE'S HIS TRANS-PHOBIA AND ON THE OTHER, THERE'S MY EXISTENCE AS A TRANS WOMAN?
HELLO?
I WAS SHOCKED AND HURT TO HEAR SO MUCH RESISTANCE FROM

NOBODY IN THE FAMILY WILL SPEAK UP FOR YOU.
... SAID SHE WOULD...
HEARING SUCH A BITTER ATTITUDE FROM A PERSON WHO LOVINGLY RAISED ME SHOOK ME TO MY CORE.

IT'S ON ME TO FIX THE SITUATION AFTER I HAD THE AUDACITY TO COME OUT, IS IT??
TYPE TYPE TYPE
MY ANGER AND ANXIETY DROVE ME TO SEND A MESSAGE.

APRIL 10, 2019

APRIL 11, 2019

ANXIOUS ABOUT THE SITUATION, I WAS UP WITH INSOMNIA ALL NIGHT...

I CAN'T BELIEVE I WAS TOLD BY MY PARENTS THAT MY FEELINGS AND EXPERIENCES DON'T MATTER???

I HONESTLY DIDN'T SEE THIS LACK OF SUPPORT COMING AND... **IT HURTS.**

APRIL 13, 2019

APRIL 14, 2019

APRIL 15, 2019

APRIL 16, 2019

APRIL 18, 2019

APRIL 19, 2019

APRIL 20, 2019

APRIL 21, 2019

APRIL 22, 2019

APRIL 23, 2019

APRIL 24, 2019

APRIL 25, 2019

APRIL 26, 2019

APRIL 27, 2019

APRIL 28, 2019

APRIL 29, 2019

APRIL 30, 2019

MAY 1, 2019

MR BLUE SKY~
PLEASE TELL US WHY~
IT'S SO WEIRD HOW YOU CAN PASS BY SOMONE AT PARTIES

HOW DO YOU FEEL ABOUT OVERALLS?
LIKE THEY'RE OVERSIZED CHILDREN'S CLOTHES!!
RIGHT??
TIME AND TIME AGAIN AND NOT EVEN REALIZE

IN CONCLUSION, BUGS: I WANNA EAT 'EM!!
I'M TWEETING THIS RIGHT NOW.
THEY WERE A GOOD FRIEND LYING IN WAIT ALL ALONG.

WHAT IF SHE'S JUST A NATURALLY TOUCHY PERSON AND JUST MAKING ME A PLAYLIST TO CEMENT OUR NEW FRIENDSHIP AND ALSO THAT WINKY EMOJI AFTERWARD WAS JUST HER BEING CUTE????????

ALL THAT **AND** SHE SENT YOU A **WINKY??** JULIA, LISTEN TO YOURSELF!!

I'M SO BAD AT THIS, DAVE!!

MAY 3, 2019

KRISTINE SENT ME THE PLAYLIST
IF YOU WANNA MAKE A MOVE
IF I HAD MY WAY
COME ON
I WOULD BE YOURS~
PART OF ME IS STILL CONVINCED SHE'S JUST BEING FRIENDLY.

JULIA DRAWS ME FLAT, BUT I DON'T
REALLY LOOK LIKE THAT, PAPER MUSCLES
CLOSE THE DOOR, I WATCH HER
LIKE
I CAN'T FATHOM SOMEONE LIKE HER WANTING ANYTHING MORE.

OHHHHH PRETTY DARLING~
THIS FEELING IS DEEP
INSIIIDE~
YA GOT
ME MYSTIFIED~
BUT... MY HEART. MAYBE FOR A MOMENT, I CAN PRETEND...

MAY 4, 2019

OHH, YOU REALLY LIKE THIS GIRL, HUH?

WAIT, WHAT?

YOU KEEP BLUSHING WHILE TALKING ABOUT HER...

YOU NEVER DO THAT.

N-NO I'M NOT!!

IT'S CUTE.

...SHE'S REALLY COOL.

MAY 5, 2019

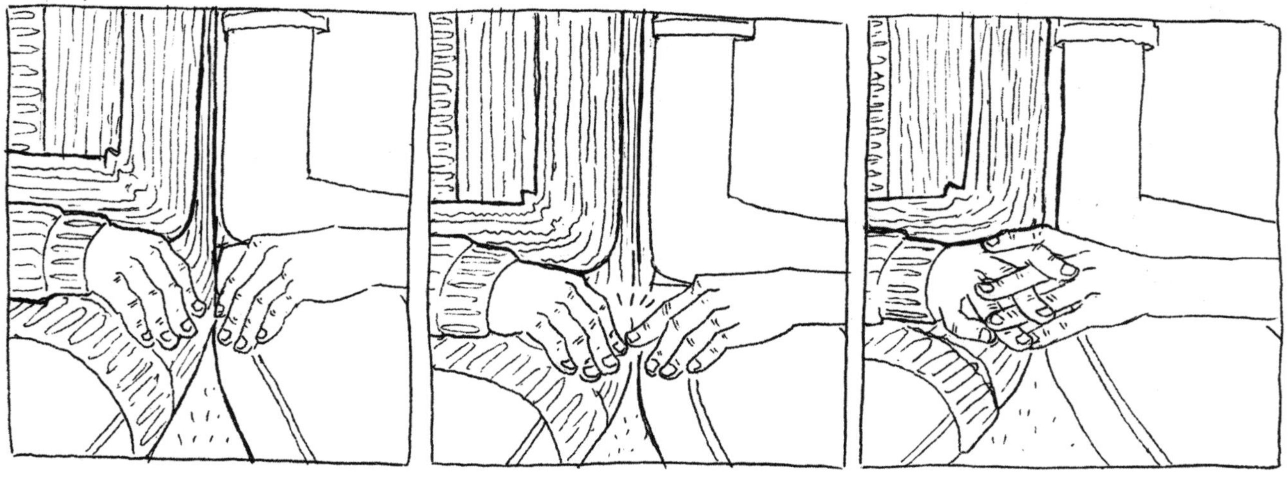

MAY 6, 2019

WORK LUNCH CREW
THE WORLD FEELS A LITTLE BRIGHTER TODAY.

TAP TAPPA TAP
WANNA GO TO A CRAFTS FAIR ON FRIDAY?
YES, PLEASE!!
DESPITE MY NERVES THAT I DON'T KNOW WHAT I WANT.

DESPITE MY FEARS THAT I'LL ONLY END UP HURT AGAIN.

MAY 7, 2019

I REALLY WANNA TEXT HER BUT I HAVE NO REAL REASON TO...IS IT TOO MUCH TO JUST ASK HOW SHE'S DOING? I DON'T WANNA OVER-DO IT AND SCARE HER OFF SO SOON INTO ALL THIS BUT I DON'T KNOW MAYBE IT'S FINE BUT THEN AGAIN WHO'S EVEN TO SAY IF SHE IS

HI HI HOPE YOU'RE HAVING A GOOD DAY TODAY!! FRIDAY SEEMS SO FAR AWAY... ARE YOU FREE AT ALL TOMORROW?
BZZT
BZZT

TAP
TAPPA
TAP
YES, ABSOLUTELY!
GOOD LORD I'M A DUMMY.
I'M REALLY ALL IN, AREN'T I?

MAY 8, 2019

I'D FORGOTTEN HOW EASY IT CAN BE TO CONNECT WITH ANOTHER PERSON.

HA HA HA HA HA HA
HA HA HA HA HA
HA HA
HA HA HA HA
HA HA HA
CRACKING JOKES NEITHER OF US WILL REMEMBER...

JUST A WONDERFUL FEELING LEFT IN THE WAKE OF IT ALL.

MAY 9, 2019

MAY 11, 2019

I JUST... CAN'T BELIEVE
IT'S HAPPENING AGAIN.

IT'S ALL SO FAMILIAR, YET IT
STILL FEELS SO FRESH, SO NEW.

I KNOW I'VE BEEN HURT BEFORE,
BUT NONE OF THAT SEEMS TO
MATTER RIGHT NOW.

MAY 12, 2019

HERE'S SOME WATER... WANNA TALK ABOUT IT?
...REMEMBER THOSE CALLS HOME I MADE A MONTH AGO?
I'M SO FORTUNATE

THERE, THERE... LET IT ALL OUT...
TH-THANK Y-YOU...
TO HAVE FRIENDS TO LEAN ON

I'M SO GLAD YOU'RE FEELING BETTER! YOU'RE TOO WONDERFUL OF A PERSON TO FEEL BAD, I WILL **NOT** ALLOW IT! I'M PUTTING MY FOOT DOWN.
WHEN LIFE BECOMES TOO MUCH.

MAY 15, 2019

I'M ON A CROSS-COUNTRY FLIGHT TO VISIT MY EX AMY FOR A WEEK
ZZZ
ZZZ
WONDERFUL AS THINGS HAVE BEEN WITH KRISTINE, DEEP-SEATED FEARS ARE STARTING TO CREEP IN.

SHE MADE ME ANOTHER PLAYLIST
IF I'M TOTALLY HONEST, STARTING A NEW RELATIONSHIP IS TERRIFYING...

I DON'T HARDLY KNOW HER
BUT I THINK I COULD LOVE HER
CRIMSON AND CLOVER~
WHAT IF THERE'S SOMETHING I DON'T SEE AND WE BOTH JUST END UP HURT BECAUSE OF IT?

MAY 16, 2019

JUST A COUPLE'A BOOBS OUT IN THE WORLD!!
BOOBIN' ALONG, AS WE DO!
IT'S WILD TO BE HANGING WITH AMY FOUR YEARS LATER.

DORKY DANCING IN A STORE
IT'S LIKE STEPPING BACK IN TIME...

GOT SOME SAUCE COMING UP!
YEA, GIRL! BRING DAT SAUS~!
EXCEPT THIS TIME AROUND, I HAVE NO SHAME ABOUT WHO I AM.

MAY 18, 2019

I'M JUST... SO FORTUNATE TO HAVE AMY IN MY LIFE.
I FEEL THAT.

THE CONCEPT OF CHOSEN FAMILY KEEPS COMING UP IN MY LIFE. I LOVE IT SO MUCH.

WHAT DO YOU SAY TO TIA AMY AND AUNT JULIE?
THANK YOU!

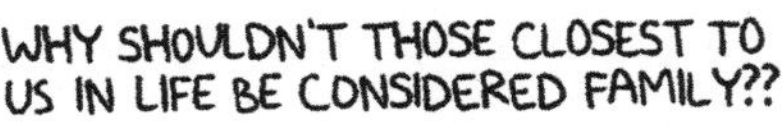
WHY SHOULDN'T THOSE CLOSEST TO US IN LIFE BE CONSIDERED FAMILY??

I'M SO GLAD I MADE TIME TO COME OUT HERE. Y'ALL ARE SO IMPORTANT TO ME.
LATELY IT'S BEEN FEELING MORE AND MORE RELEVANT ALL THE TIME.

MAY 19, 2019

WH-
SHE WROTE ME A **SONG!!** MY HEART CAN ONLY TAKE **SO MUCH!!**
LIKE, WHAT EVEN **IS** GENDER, YOU KNOW??
NOT A **SINGLE** CLUE, MY DUDE.
G'BYE AUNT JULIE!!
SEE YA AROUND, KNOX!

MAY 20, 2019

WAS MY ASSESMENT OF YOU WRONG? TOO MEAN??

NO? I MEAN, YOU'RE RIGHT IN A WAY...

I'M... I'M **NOT** CONFIDENT IN **MOST** AREAS OF MY LIFE... I TRY'N FAKE IT... A **LOT**.

THE THING IS, I NEVER WANT A LACK OF CONFIDENCE TO STOP ME FROM DOING THE THINGS I WANNA DO.

MAY 21, 2019

SO, JULIA... HOW DO YOU FEEL ABOUT THE TERM GIRLFRIEND?
IT'S CONFUSING WHEN STRAIGHT WOMEN USE IT FOR THEIR FRIENDS!
AND WHAT IF I USED IT TO REFER TO **YOU**?
HM...
I LIKE IT. IT SOUNDS NICE!
"MY GIRLFRIEND JULIA" HAS A NICE RING TO IT.

MAY 22, 2019

SHE'S THE FIRST GAY CIS WOMAN I'VE DATED... I TRY TO NOT GET SELF-CONSCIOUS ABOUT IT, BUT...
I DUNNO, I GUESS IT'S INTERNALIZED TRANSPHOBIA...
I **KNOW** SHE SEES ME AS A WOMAN, BUT AT THE SAME TIME, IT'S LIKE, WHY WOULD SHE CHOOSE TO BE WITH **ME** OVER A CIS WOMAN?
I'M SO... INSECURE.
YOU JUST SAID IT YOURSELF, SHE'S WITH YOU BECAUSE SHE SEES YOU AS THE LOVELY WOMAN YOU ARE.
YEAHHH, YOU RIGHT...

MAY 23, 2019

OK OK OK DON'T PANIC JULIE. SHE'S COMIN' OVER ON SATURDAY. GOT A LOT OF TIME TO FILL.
GOD, WHAT DO PEOPLE EVEN **DO**??
HMMM MMMMM MMMMM MMM...
FARMER'S MARKET! YES!! THAT'S TOTALLY A DATE-LIKE THING!!
THAT'S A START!!

MAY 25, 2019

GOOD MORNING~
G'MORNIN'...
I'M TRYING TO BE PRAGMATIC, KEEP AN EYE OUT FOR RED FLAGS,

THIS IS GONNA BE MY OUTFIT WHEN I'M IN GAY BABY JAIL!
CHEF'S KISS
BUT IT'S THE STRANGEST THING-
I DON'T SEEM TO SEE ANY WITH HER.

LEMME WARM YOUR HANDS..
OH~ THANK YOU!
THIS IS THE GAYEST I'VE EVER SEEN.
I DIDN'T KNOW DATING COULD BE THIS EASY AND CUTE.

MAY 26, 2019
A RAINY GRAY AND SLEEPY DAY
MONTHS HAVE PASSED. MY FEELINGS REGARDING LIV ARE MUCH LESS RAW.
HEY, WANNA CATCH UP?
TAP TAPPA TAP
YEAH!!
WHILE I'M NOT SURE I'M READY TO HAVE HER BACK IN MY LIFE YET,
I STILL CARE ABOUT HER.
I WANNA KNOW HOW SHE'S BEEN.

MAY 27, 2019

OH GOD, I'M SORRY... WE WERE HAVING A FUN TIME. I DON'T MEAN TO WRECK IT BY CRYING...
NO NO NO, IT'S OK...
I JUST, SPENT SO MUCH OF MY CHILDHOOD NOT ALLOWING MYSELF TO ENJOY THINGS I WOULD'VE OTHERWISE LOVED OUT OF SHAME.
IT MAKES IT HARD TO HAVE FUN, LIGHTHEARTED CONVERSATIONS ABOUT BEING A KID. I'M SO SORRY.
IT'S OK... I UNDERSTAND.

MAY 28, 2019

I THINK I'M ON THE MEND, MY THROAT'S STARTING TO FEEL BETTER
AW YAY, I'M SO GLAD~
WAIT A SECOND... M-MY THROAT!!
OH NO.
OH MY GOD. I CAN'T BELIEVE KISSING WOULD EVER BETRAY ME.

MAY 29, 2019

GUHHHH... I CAN'T BELIEVE I FINALLY CAUGHT THAT BUG THAT'S BEEN GOIN' AROUND...
THIS KEEPS GETTING WORSE AND WORSE...
NOOOO I WANNA HOLD U AND BRING U GINGER ALE
TAP TAPPA TAP
GUHHH... I FEEL LIKE I'M DYING WHYYY
I'M ALWAYS HERE FOR U, WHATEVER U NEED
TAP TAPPA TAP
SHE'S SO WONDERFUL... IT'S SO NICE TO NOT FEEL ALONE.

MAY 31, 2019

HIII~ HOW YA FEELIN' TODAY?
DOIN' SO MUCH BETTER!
YESSSS!!!!
TAP
TAPPA
TAP
GOOD MORNIN'
TEXTS
YOU KNOW, I'D ALWAYS HEARD
THAT IT SHOULD BE EASY.

HEY! QUICK Q! SHOULD I TAKE A DAY
OFF FOR THE CARLY RAE SHOW?
YEAH! HERE'S WHAT
I WAS THINKING...
MAKING PLANS
IS SO EASY AND
SIMPLE
BUT I NEVER UNDERSTOOD
EXACTLY WHAT THAT MEANT

HEYYY~
YOU'RE REALLY
CUTE AND I
MISS YOU
BZZ!
AND HOW MUCH IT'D MEAN
FOR MY PEACE OF MIND.

JUNE 1, 2019

I HAD INSOMNIA LAST NIGHT.
LIFE STRESS FOLLOWED ME TO BED.

THE MOUNTAIN OF THINGS THAT NEED DOING JUST KEEPS RISING HIGHER AND HIGHER.

I FEEL AS THOUGH I'M WORKING HARDER THAN I EVER HAVE AND GETTING ABSOLUTELY NOWHERE.

JUNE 2, 2019

SINCE STARTING TO DATE
ANOTHER QUEER PERSON,

I'VE STARTED FEELING FREER
IN MY EXPRESSION OF GENDER...

HECK
YES.
FEELING LESS FEAR OF JUDGMENT FOR
APPEARING LESS TYPICALLY FEMININE.

JUNE 3, 2019

I HAD A FUN TIME TONIGHT!
SAME! ONCE PAST THE INITIAL AWKWARDNESS, SO DID I. I'M GLAD YOU'RE WELL, LIV!
SO... HOW YA FEELIN' ABOUT, Y'KNOW, FRIENDSHIP, MOVING FORWARD?
IT'S... HARD TO SAY? I'LL NEED TIME TO PROCESS TONIGHT.
THAT'S FAIR. YOU LET ME KNOW.
I WILL. THANKS FOR UNDERSTANDING.

JUNE 5, 2019

I'M STILL NOT ENTIRELY SURE WHAT FOLKS SEE WHEN THEY LOOK AT ME.

HAVE YOU BEEN HELPED YET?
"PASSING" IS SUCH A FRAUGHT CONCEPT, I HAVE NO IDEA IF I READ AS TRANS.

OH, SHE WAS HERE FIRST.
THANK YOU!
BUT I'M USUALLY PERCEIVED TO BE A WOMAN AND THAT RULES.

JUNE 6, 2019

CHILDHOOD
UGHH
EXHAUSTION
TIME
MONEY
FAMILY
WORK
SADNESS
DYSPHORIA

OH HEY! I FOLLOW YOU ONLINE! YOUR WORK HAS REALLY HELPED MY TRANS FRIENDS! MIND IF WE TAKE A PICTURE TOGETHER?
OH! ER, SURE??

CLICK!
OH, RIGHT. MY LIFE MAY BE FAR FROM PERFECT, BUT I'M MAKING THE MOST OF THE TIME I HAVE.

JUNE 7, 2019

JUNE 8, 2019

KINDA WILD THAT I ENDED UP IN A RELATIONSHIP WITH A GIRL AGAIN AFTER BEING SO BOY CRAZY LATELY.

DESPITE MY DIFFICULTIES IN DATING MEN, I'M GLAD I HAD SOME TIME TO EXPLORE THAT SIDE OF MYSELF.

I MISSED YOU.
I MISSED YOU TOO.
I'M PAN AND QUEER AND THAT'S ALL THERE IS TO IT.

JUNE 9, 2019

BYE CUTIES!! DO GOOD WORK~!
YOU TOO! GOODBYE JULIA!!
IN THE FUTURE, HOW AM I GOING TO LOOK BACK ON THIS PERIOD?

HM... COULD I EVER SUPPORT MYSELF AS A CARTOONST...? I WONDER...
I HOPE I DON'T JUDGE MYSELF TOO HARSHLY. I DID THE BEST I COULD.

HOW YA DOIN', RAYE?
HEY JULIAAA!
LIFE IS MESSY, BUT I TRY MY BEST. ALWAYS HAVE, ALWAYS WILL.

epilogue

That's not the end, of course, just a stopping point.

It's a funny thing, being able to look back at this stretch of time in my life laid out so plainly. Despite having felt completely lost at the time, this collection reads as though I went through a defined character arc: I'd started out in the comfort of a long-term (albeit doomed) relationship, went through a breakup, dealt with the throes of the grieving and healing processes, made futile attempts at dating, and then ended up happily in a positive, affirming relationship.

That aspect of the narrative is so neat and tidily wrapped up with a bow, you almost expect to turn the last page to see "and she lived happily ever after. The end." That sorta thing. But real life isn't as cut-and-dried as all that. The story of my life kept on going and, as I sit here writing this nine months later, it already feels like so much has happened and changed.

For instance, though my relationship with Kristine was important for a number of reasons, we have since amicably split up and I have gone on to date other people. I've drifted apart from some of the friendships I had at the time and have grown closer in others. I've been through emotionally difficult events that required me to fight to prevent those experiences from hardening my heart. But I've also enjoyed so many incredible moments that have served as countless reminders of just how amazing it is to be alive. And on and on. Life is complex and unexpected in endless ways.

At its core, this series is about the importance of all the small moments that make up the greater whole that is my life as an adult queer woman. I may be a woman who came into herself later in life than most, but I'm doing what I can with the time I've been given. The point is that I exist and I'm out here making the most of the life I have.

—Julia

afterword: setting aside past regrets

Note: Throughout the following text I refer to my pre-transition self as a man and use he/him/his pronouns. While it felt right for me to do so for creative purposes in the context of this afterword, please, when discussing my past, present, and future: always use she/her pronouns and refer to me as a woman. Thank you.

A few years back, when I had just started on the path toward self-acceptance and began the hard work of growing into the person I wanted to become, a division began to grow between who I was before starting my transition and after. As I began focusing on my future, I found myself mentally and emotionally distancing from the person I used to be.

And of course I did: I was feeling an excitement for life I had never before known! My life suddenly felt full of possibility—there was so much to take in and so many new experiences I wanted to have! I couldn't *wait* for the world to recognize me as myself, as Julia! But along with the knowledge that a better life for myself was attainable came resentment toward the person I had been Before.

Despite having lived *as* him for the prior twenty-seven years, I began to view him as an almost separate entity from myself. I thought of him as nothing more than the sad shell of a man I happened to share memories with; a deeply repressed person who bore an unfortunate familial resemblance to me. And as time went on, I grew to loathe him.

Because the thing is, once I finally accepted that I was trans and needed to do something about it, all the dysphoria and depression I'd always lived with became *painfully* obvious in retrospect. They bled into practically every aspect of my life! How could he have missed the signs?? I felt betrayed that he didn't see them for what they were earlier and felt immense regret for how much of my life was wasted as someone wandering around lost, passively swaying along with the forces of societal expectations. I couldn't believe how long he had aimlessly let other people's ideas push him around this way and that, as he tried to fall in line with whatever and whoever he thought he was supposed to be.

I became so angry that my youth had been stolen from me and there was *nothing* I could do about it. All that wasted time I could never get back! It hurt so much that I never got to be the little girl I should've been, or the teen I could've been. I had missed out on so many life experiences that I'd never have the opportunity to participate in again. I felt powerless; tied to the dead weight of my past life.

I *hated* it. I hated it so much. I hated *him* so much.

But the longer I've lived as a more complete version of myself, the more time I've had to process these feelings, and have since come to realize that I'd been looking at it all wrong. I'd been so wrapped up in my newfound identity and zest for life that I had *completely* disregarded his side of the story and swept aside *his* feelings throughout it all.

I've started to better understand and really connect with the idea that when I look back on our shared memories and feel our shared emotions, I'm looking at someone who was struggling to survive. I see a person who was *deeply* in pain, anxious, and scared; trying his best to just hold on. A person who kept on going, blindly carrying the hope that one day life may get better, despite never having any evidence that would ever be the case. This was someone who didn't even know that being trans was something that one *could* be. And yet, despite the hurt, despite the confusion, despite everything, he kept moving forward. The sheer might of his willpower is stunning to me. And in acknowledging all this, how can I feel anything but compassion for him? His existence was nothing short of *beautiful*.

All that time I felt I'd lost? I get it now. He hadn't stolen my past at all—*he had protected my future*. The emotional walls he'd built to keep himself safe? They were what allowed Julia to one day thrive. I have so much admiration for his ability to put one foot in front of the next. From where I now stand, it's hard to fathom just how much strength it had taken for him to even begin to open himself up after the life he lived, feeling entirely, impossibly alone in the world.

And I carry that strength with me now; that indomitable spirit, now unshackled from the crushing weight of dysphoria. The reason I've been able to grow and take charge of my life in ways I never could've imagined is because I know I'm capable of handling myself. Because if he could do it, *so can I*.

And the most beautiful part of it all is that his struggle wasn't in vain. As improbable as it may have then seemed, I've grown into a woman he'd have wept tears of joy to know would eventually be realized. I've become the girl he thought could only ever exist in his most secretive daydreams. I'm openly, unabashedly myself now and it's *everything* he ever hoped it would be.

The truth is, and I now know this deep in my heart, that things never could've played out any other way. I couldn't have embraced my reality as Julia any earlier than I had. That I was able to at all is an absolute *gift*.

I'm able to love myself now. All of me. And for that I'll be forever grateful.

about the author

Julia Kaye is an award-winning artist and illustrator whose autobiographical webcomic, *Up and Out,* has garnered hundreds of thousands of readers and wide critical praise. Her commitment to activism has led to collaborations with non-profit organizations such as The Trevor Project and Trans Lifeline. Her work has appeared on Webtoon, GoComics, BuzzFeed, and the Disney animated show *Big City Greens*. Julia lives in Los Angeles.

My Life in Transition copyright © 2021 by Julia Kaye. All rights reserved.
Printed in China. No part of this book may be used or reproduced in
any manner whatsoever without written permission except
in the case of reprints in the context of reviews.

Andrews McMeel Publishing
a division of Andrews McMeel Universal
1130 Walnut Street, Kansas City, Missouri 64106

www.andrewsmcmeel.com

21 22 23 24 25 SDB 10 9 8 7 6 5 4 3 2 1

ISBN: 978-1-5248-6046-2

Library of Congress Control Number: 2020942204

Editor: Allison Adler
Art Director: Holly Swayne
Production Editor: Margaret Daniels
Production Manager: Chuck Harper

ATTENTION: SCHOOLS AND BUSINESSES
Andrews McMeel books are available at quantity discounts with
bulk purchase for educational, business, or sales promotional use.
For information, please e-mail the Andrews McMeel Publishing
Special Sales Department: specialsales@amuniversal.com.